IT TAKES MORE THAN LEGS TO
Stand

Lyla Swafford

Many Blessings

Lyla S.

To my parents

and daughter Rachael

and many others who have

encouraged me to stand and walk.

CONTENTS

Chapter 1

I **could see fear in my nine-year-old daughter's eyes** as she repeated the question for the third time. "Mom, *why* do you want to go parasailing?"

I smiled and then laughed. "Honey, it'll be fun!" Although Rachael loves adventure, she was afraid because I have Cerebral Palsy and often have trouble keeping my balance when I walk. In addition, I can't open my right hand and have limited use of my left.

Rachael and I were visiting my family in Montana. My sister Karen heard my enthusiasm and put together the plans to make it happen. Along with her daughter Danita, we packed up and set out for the cabin owned by Karen's friend, Julie. Julie would join us on this adventure as well.

About the time the girls got tired of riding in the van, Karen found Julie's cabin, just five minutes from the lakeside park. That night as we sat eating pizza around Julie's fireplace, Rachael snuggled close to me. "Hey Mom, can I ride horses tomorrow?" I remembered passing a sign advertising a riding stable not far from the cabin. Danita chimed in: "I want to go too!" So, after breakfast the next morning, we piled in the van and headed for the stables.

After the girls finished horseback riding, we stopped at a nearby lake and took a boat ride. My excitement grew as I realized that my dream—parasailing—was also a possibility for me.

"That's the adventure I'd like to have!" I told Karen excitedly. She spoke to the owners, describing my limitations. "Is there any way Lyla can go parasailing?"

"If someone goes with her, she'll be perfectly safe," the owner assured her.

When Karen finished talking to the owner, she came over to me with a big smile on her face.

"So, do you really want to go parasailing?" she asked.

I squealed with delight.

Steve, the boat owner, explained to us that the person in back needed full control of his or her hands. Then he told me, "All you have to do is enjoy your ride!"

Julie spoke up. "I've wanted to parasail for a long time, Lyla. Can I be your partner?"

I laughed, "Absolutely."

As Steve held up the coil of rope in his hands, my heart pounded with excitement. "We use this to maneuver the parasail," he explained, then turned to Julie. "I'll use arm signals to communicate with you. When you see my arm go up, I want you to pull your rope tight. Lyla, Julie will sit behind you and help guide the parasail so you can have a great time."

With Rachael and Danita in tow, Steve walked ahead to prepare his boat. Since my balance is so poor, Karen and Julie took a firm grip of each arm, helping me walk down the dock and get into Steve's boat. After we settled in our seats, Steve surprised Rachael by saying, "Do you want to help steer?"

Rachael jumped out of her seat and reached for the wheel. Soon, the boat was skimming across the water, circling the lake. Rachael grinned at me. As Julie wiggled into the harness, Karen put the legs of my own harness over my feet. I stood up and leaned on her and she pulled it up to my waist. When Julie and I were both ready, Steve slowed the motor, and Julie hopped over the side of the boat and into the water.

Karen steadied me as I stood up. I reached out for Julie and let her pull me into the water. It was so cold I coughed and tried to catch my breath. When my sister finished making all the necessary adjustments to my harness, the boat picked up speed and pulled away from us. As it did, our pink and white parasail began to rise, taking us in the air with it!

I was bursting with excitement as I soared higher and higher into the air. Usually, I was the one watching others perform daring feats, but this time they were watching me! My disability wasn't holding me back! I looked down at the boat and saw Rachael, her upturned face mirroring the delight in my own. I felt completely alone with God and at peace as we soared through the blue skies above Flathead Lake. Now I knew how it felt to be in the shelter of God's wings.

That was a perfect day. For one day, for a few moments of it, I could feel free. I had longed for this feeling, this freedom, all of my life. From the day I was born, my parents had no idea I could ever experience this kind of adventure. Their original dreams for my future had been buried long ago.

Chapter 2

In **April 1951, signs of new life were everywhere** on my parents' Montana farm. As excited as they were to see the spring wheat break through the rich soil, they eagerly looked forward to an even greater event—the birth of their first child.

My mother's water broke after a Sunday chicken supper. It was sixty miles to the nearest hospital in Havre, Montana. Mom was in agony all the way and was taken to the delivery room when she arrived. It didn't take long for the nurses to determine there was trouble ahead. Mother could hear them calling several doctors frantically. Since they were changing shifts, the nurses all stayed to help.

At Mom's last doctor's appointment, the doctor determined that I hadn't turned in the position to be born. So, with his nurse on one side of me and the doctor on the other, they manipulated me into the right position for birth.

That night, Mom was up walking the floor in pain. "Since I'd never had a baby before, I thought maybe I was in labor, but the pain eventually subsided."

My parents got to the hospital around ten thirty on a Sunday night. The nurses called my doctor and he told them to get someone else because it was his weekend off. My mom heard them frantically calling several doctors in the area. Two doctors answered the call.

Mom could watch the birth in a mirror. Being young and uninformed, when she saw the white, fluffy cord coming out, she thought she'd have her baby soon. But her legs in the stirrups suddenly began to shake and her knees began to knock. Although she didn't realize it, she'd gone into shock.

"I heard myself screaming and they held my head while they gave me ether," Mom remembers. After an intense battle to save my life I was finally born. Mom remembers that I was beautiful except for the brownish bruise around my neck, caused from the umbilical cord being wrapped very tightly around my neck.

Later, Mom and Dad learned that the umbilical cord had been wrapped around my neck very tightly. My exhausted doctor finally walked into the hospital's waiting room to talk with my father. "It's a girl," he said, and then added a deep sigh. "It was the toughest delivery I have ever had."

Ten days later, he stopped to see my mother when he was making his rounds. "Both of you have had a hard time," he commented. "But you can take your daughter home. I think she'll be fine." Mom and Dad were delighted and relieved.

During the early months, however, Mom became increasingly worried about me. Since I wasn't learning to sit up, she propped me in a cardboard box and placed blankets around me. When she questioned the doctor, he said I was just slow. Thinking back, she believes that kind old doctor just didn't want to tell her that I had all the symptoms of Cerebral Palsy: clamped fists, arched back.

When Mom heard a specialist from Great Falls was coming to Havre, she made an appointment for me. She was hopeful she would find out some answers to her questions.

At my appointment the specialist played games with me while he performed an examination. There was compassion in his voice when he finally spoke. "I'm sorry to have to tell you this, but your daughter has Cerebral Palsy."

"Cerebral Palsy?"

My parents had never even heard of it!

Mom returned to the clinic because she was pregnant again. By this time, Mom was worn out and weighed only a hundred pounds. She was close to a breakdown.

I was two years old when my brother was born. I was used to being the center of mom's universe. "You resented your baby brother when he was born," Mom told me. "Whenever I nursed Gary, you'd wheel up to me in your walker and lay your head on my lap and cry as though your heart was broken. You cried all through his bath, making me more of a nervous wreck than I was already."

Since I couldn't sit up when other babies did, Mom sat with me on the floor and propped me against the cupboards. Then she'd turn the pages of a book to see how long I could sit up before I tumbled over. She put paper in my bassinet to get me to kick and set me in a cardboard box to play, propped up by pillows.

Friends helped my parents make arrangements for me to be examined by a doctor at the Shriners Hospital in Spokane, Washington. Mom remembers being up most of the night before we left for Shriners. She said, "I was afraid they'd want you to stay. Instead, they said there was nothing they could do, so we went back home."

Chapter 3

My mother's relatives from Canada lived near the physical therapy center, so we could stay with them when I had to go for therapy and checkups. My Grandmother could take care of my new baby brother while Mom took me for my regular routine.

When we were there, the therapists taught mom how to help me do my exercises at home between appointments. Although I made progress, my parents were told I'd do better if I could see a therapist regularly. They struggled to find a way they could meet my needs and continue farming. Their search led them to the Montana Center for Cerebral Palsy and Handicapped Children in Billings. A few weeks later, my parents went on a tour of the facility with Principal Johnson.

They were impressed because it was like a small community providing a wide range of services to help each child. As they finished their tour, my Dad told the principal, "It seems like our daughter would really benefit from going here, but it's so far away from my farm."

Mr. Johnson agreed and took out the school calendar, "Classes start September third."

Dad looked at him, "We won't be able to get her here until I finish the work on our farm."

"I understand," Mr. Johnson replied. "But it'll be better if she can start school on time."

"Do you have any ideas?" Mom wanted to know.

"If I can find another family to take care of her for a while, would you consider it?"

Tears welled up in her eyes. "She's only four."

Mom's heart was torn with the thought of leaving me in the care of others, but she wanted so much for me to have every opportunity to develop. She sighed reluctantly, and then said, "But I suppose so."

Dad tried to comfort Mom. "We won't leave her with anyone very long. I think she'll be okay."

The principal told my parents that one of the aides at the school had actually taken care of handicapped children in her home. After they met Mrs. Louk and her family, they felt much better. When the arrangements were made, I moved in with them and started school. They were good to me, but I missed my home and parents—especially Mom tucking me into bed at night.

My parents felt it was important to keep our family together. So, after the fall work on the farm, they packed up their household and came to live with me. In the springtime, the routine was reversed.

I enjoyed being with other kids who were like me at school. After the occupational therapists taught me how to use my crippled hand to feed and dress myself, I did it at home, too. I continued to go there until my parents found another school only two hours from our home.

Every few months, doctors came to our school to check each of us to see whether our physical and occupational therapies were helping us. I always tried to walk my best, but I was never able to fool them. I was seven years old when, as I finished doing my therapy walk for the doctors, one of them told my parents, "Her ankles are rolling out. She'll have more stability if we take her shin bones and put them in her ankles."

Surgery was scheduled. I became really scared and thought I would suffocate when they covered my face with a horrible smelling mask. I twisted my head to get away, but I was no match for the doctor. Soon I was asleep. Hours later, I awoke with both of my legs in casts up to my knees. Mom and Dad stayed with me the rest of the day.

The next morning, Mom's eyes blazed as she caught a nurse walking me back to bed from the bathroom. "Lyla just had a bone

graft on both of her legs. The doctor ordered her to use a bedpan."
After they helped me back in bed, and I finally stopped crying
because I was in such pain, Mom called the doctor and reported
what the nurse had done to me.

At the end of a very long summer, I was really excited about
finally getting my casts off. But the loud sound of the electric saw
terrified me and I squirmed to get away. "You're cutting me," I
screamed. When the doctor saw blood on my leg, he frowned.
"That wouldn't have happened if you had laid still!"

After the casts were taken off, my therapists and I began the
painful process of stretching my tightened muscles. Unlike the
doctor who removed my casts, the therapists were sensitive. But
the surgery left long, ugly scars on my legs. Later, in my preteen
and teenage years, I felt very self-conscious whenever I wore
dresses or shorts. Even though very few people asked about them, I
was sure they were the first things they saw.

I could cover up my scars by wearing slacks and the scars
faded over time, but the pain of perceived rejection and judgment
continued to fester in my heart

When my Uncle Roy from California came to visit, he asked
dad, "How's Lyla doing in the new school?"

"Well, it's better for the rest of the family because we don't
have to move since it's close enough for Lyla to come home on

weekends."

Uncle Roy looked thoughtful. "Yeah. That would make things easier."

"But, to be honest, the other school may have met her needs better," Dad said. "She doesn't seem to be learning as much and her walking is worse. Elaine and I just aren't sure what to do."

Roy responded, "There's a school near where we live that would be ideal. Let's see if she can go there. We'd really like to play a role in seeing that Lyla gets all the help she needs."

Since they wanted me to get the best treatment possible as well, my parents, along with my paternal grandparents, took me to California to live with my aunt and uncle. When the first day of school was over, I could hardly wait to tell Mom what happened! But my heart sunk as I got "home" and remembered my parents were on their way back to Montana. The California heat along with the shrieking sounds of my cousin's violin intensified my homesickness. I went outside and cried. My ten-year-old heart felt incredibly alone.

Once I got used to the living arrangements, I liked my new school and all the new places I could go. My cousin Alice, helped me with my homework and read to me at bedtime. But when my Dad called and said, "Honey, how would you like to come home for Christmas," I was so excited all I could do was squeal! My excitement mounted as my classmates and I practiced for our Christmas program. I knew the day after school was out I'd be going home!

I was only ten, so flying all by myself made me feel like a "big girl." The weather added to the excitement when a blizzard greeted us as the plane entered Montana. For a while, the lights were out at the airport. Mom went through her own turbulence when she heard the announcement, "Due to weather conditions, this flight won't be able to land. " She was relieved when the lights came on and we were cleared for landing. Practically everyone had gotten airsick—including me. But, despite my messy condition, I was greeted with lots of hugs!

It was wonderful to play with my brothers and little sister and eat the Christmas treats Mom had made. But all too soon it was time for me to go back California to finish the school year. I was sick a lot of the rest of the year, and my parents decided I was too young to be so far away from home.

For the next few years my parents moved our family to California so we could be together while I went to school. I stayed with foster families when my Dad needed to be at the farm. Mom did her best to support me during this time of separation, but sometimes I just couldn't cope.

Finally the happy day came and my parents and I were told I no longer had to attend the "special school." I was very excited about going to public school because I thought it meant I was *normal*. It didn't take too long for reality to set in. I felt that I was was less normal than ever. Even with only twelve students in my seventh grade class, I was the brunt of many of their jokes. One day, I overheard some of them talking about my ugly shoes. I didn't cry, but I sure let Mom know how I felt when I got home.

It was very difficult for me to keep up with my homework. Even with Mom's help, I worried about my grades so much I became physically sick.

The year wasn't all work and no play, though. I loved being part of the pep-club and cheering when my brothers played basketball. I also enjoyed going to the show with my family on weekends.

As a child, the seeds of faith had been planted in my young heart by Sunday School teachers and the women who led a Good News Club in my neighborhood. Faith was further cultivated when I met with my pastor to prepare for confirmation. As a teenager, I loved sharing with my girlfriends and my youth group what Jesus was doing in my life.

Like many seniors in high school, I began to wonder what I wanted to do after I graduated. One fall afternoon, one of my friends invited me to go to a weekend retreat she was going to with her youth group. I wanted to go, but I really doubted whether Mom would let me. I had such a difficult time walking that I hadn't been able to go on other retreats. After I told Mom about the retreat and assured her that my friend Sarah would help me, she agreed. I squealed with delight when she said I could go.

Sarah and I were so excited about going to camp together it seemed like Friday would never come. When we got there, my joy overshadowed any difficulty I had walking around the campground.

After a few announcements, the pastor leading the retreat introduced the special guests: "Our speaker and worship team are from George Fox College." As the kids started to sing, I began to feel refreshed and encouraged. Everyone seemed friendly, and I felt totally accepted. While Chaplain Ron spoke Saturday afternoon, I began to wonder if God had led me to the retreat to answer my question about my future.

I knew I wanted to talk to him as soon as the meeting was over. I was so excited and the room was filled with so much teenage noise that Ron couldn't understand me. He pointed to the fireplace and said, "Let's meet over there in about twenty minutes."

As we sat down on a couch, Ron asked, "Are you doing okay up here? I can see that you have trouble walking."

"I have Cerebral Palsy so my balance isn't very good. It's a little bit more difficult to walk up here, but I'm so glad I got to come. Your teachings and the kids are awesome."

After we visited for a while I told him, "I've been praying about what to do after high school. When you were speaking, a *crazy thought* went through my mind."

Ron asked, "Oh, what was it?"

"I think I might really like going to George Fox. But I'm not sure I could handle it. Before this weekend, I didn't even know anything about the college. What do you think?"

"You're just the kind of student we want at Fox. Let's pray and ask God for His direction in your life."

I felt God had already answered my prayer by guiding me to Ron and George Fox. Yet, it seemed impossible. After we prayed together I was assured that my life was in God's hands.

When my parents picked me up after the retreat I said, "I had a great time! I really liked the speaker." Then I took a deep breath and continued, "He's from George Fox, a Christian college in Oregon. I think it sounds like a perfect place for me to go to college!"

"Honey," my Dad replied, "that's too big of a decision to make just by hearing a guy talk." Reality began to sink in as Mom added, "We've never heard of George Fox. Besides, it's a long way from home." The more I tried to convince them to check this out, the more frustrated everyone got. Pretty soon even I wondered if my plan was just a crazy idea. I didn't know how to help them see my point of view, but I couldn't just forget what I wanted to do.

This began a tug of war between God and me. Over and over again I had to release my dream to Him. Each time I did, He gave me such peace that I wondered why I'd been so worried.

A few weeks after the retreat, during a class meeting, the principal came in and asked, "Does anyone have any suggestions about who to invite to speak for your graduation?"

I raised my hand right away, "I just met someone who'd be great!"

Our principal was a bit surprised. "Who is he?"

"Ron was the speaker at a retreat I went to. He's the chaplain of George Fox College."

"This isn't a religious service," he warned. I don't want someone who's going to talk about God."

None of the other students had any recommendations so I said, "Why don't you call him?"

A few days later when I was typing in the school office the principal glanced at me as he walked by. "When you're finished come and talk to me."

I hurriedly finished my project and went to see why he wanted me. "I guess you know that I was reluctant to ask a chaplain to speak at graduation."

I nodded and sat in the chair across from his desk as he continued. "But I talked to your friend Ron this morning. He sounds like a nice guy, Lyla. I told him that you recommended him as a speaker for graduation."

My principal smiled and said, "I wanted you to be the first to know. Ron is coming to speak at graduation."

Thrilled with this answer to prayer, I went to tell my friends my wonderful news! I also finished the application for George Fox, praying that God would open the door if that was where He wanted me to go.

A few weeks after Ron spoke at graduation, I was accepted to George Fox. I moved onto the campus just a few short months later.

Like many students, I loved the social interaction of college, but my physical limitations added many challenges. My balance made walking around campus a tiresome feat and my struggle to keep up with homework was another story. Fellow classmates helped me by giving me a carbon copy of their notes. Most of time I used two fingers to type my assignments on my portable Smith Corona typewriter, but the final drafts of my term papers were typed by friends. The college prayer room was near the school cafeteria, so I frequently went in to pray for the strength to get through the day.

There were days when exhaustion and discouragement seemed bigger than my dream of graduating and helping others with disabilities live their lives to the fullest. God's promises gave me courage and, by God's grace, I inched closer and closer to graduation day!

𝒶 **school journalist took my picture and wrote** an article for both the Newberg and college newspapers because I was one of the first disabled students to graduate from George Fox. The audience applauded and tears of joy trickled down Mom's cheeks as I staggered forward to receive my college diploma. Despite what had seemed to be insurmountable odds, I had achieved my goal!

With my degree in psychology/sociology, I had high hopes of living independently and working to assist other people with disabilities. I eagerly put in job applications. When I wasn't hired, I felt rejected and thought it was because of my disability. Later, I discovered the position I was applying for required a master's degree and our country's economy was in crisis, so the job market became especially tight. My dream of being self-sufficient was headed for the cemetery. I felt ashamed and defeated when I realized my only choice was to apply for subsidized housing and Supplemental Security Income.

I was heartbroken. I'd spent four years in college in order to be a contributing member of society. Instead I had to be supported by the government. College diploma or not, no one wanted to hire a woman with Cerebral Palsy.

One afternoon I caught the bus and had dinner with friends before their Bible study. That particular evening, the director of Good Samaritan Ministries, Bettie Mitchell, came to share her testimony. My heart was stirred as she read the parable of the Good Samaritan in Luke. She emphasized that God has a purpose for each of us. That was great encouragement to me, so after the meeting I went to see her for counseling.

Bettie was instrumental to me, because I began the process of letting God heal my heart. Over the next several months, I faced my long-standing feelings of rejection and marginalization, and of failure and hopelessness. Bettie encouraged me to take off my happy face and be completely honest with God about my thoughts and feelings so He could heal my heart completely. I thought I had done that, but I learned it happens in stages.

Chapter 5

𝒶 **few months after I moved into my dark studio** apartment, I walked to the store across the street. While I was there, I chatted with one of the men I'd seen there a couple of days before. It turned out he was a neighbor of mine. I was pleasantly surprised when he asked, "It's such a beautiful day. Would you like to go for a ride with me?"

He was the first guy who had invited me to do anything, and it triggered my longing to be special to someone. I wasn't even aware of my longing for companionship.

When I got home that night, I did what many women do. I called my good friend Brenda. "Guess what! I talk to my neighbor, Glenn, at the store, and we went and spent the afternoon together."

She caught the excitement in my voice. "My goodness, Lyla, it sounds like you had a great time. What's he like?"

"He's tender-hearted, and he doesn't care that I have Cerebral Palsy."

We were together most of the time. I couldn't imagine my future without him, so when he proposed a few months later, I quickly answered, "yes!"

My parents were concerned because I had known Glenn only a short time, and he was so different than I was. At times, I saw things that troubled me in our relationship, but I ignored them. After a few months of preparation, family members from Montana and Canada gathered to celebrate at my wedding.

I went from feeling rejected by society to feeling chosen. Getting married was something I hadn't even dreamed of because women with severe disabilities aren't expected to have intimate relationships. We are perceived as asexual—as not desiring love or sex or a committed involvement. Glenn and I were attracted to one another because of the needs in both of our lives. We'd had significant struggles throughout childhood. When I asked him if he loved the Lord, he said, "Yes."

I thought the Lord told me we should get married, but it didn't take long for me to wonder if I'd heard right. Shortly after we married, his mood swings scared and confused me. All through our marriage, I hoped my positive outlook on life would rub off on him.

We didn't plan to have children because I didn't think I could care for them, yet several years later Glenn and I were ecstatic to find out I was pregnant. Friends were concerned and thought I might not be able to walk when I gained weight. Instead, after a normal and relatively easy pregnancy, I was able to walk into the hospital to have my baby.

Before my due date, my doctor and I decided that we would see if my muscles would help me deliver naturally but, if they didn't, I would need to have a C-section. On the big day my doctor wasn't there. I broke into tears when the on-call doctor said he wanted to give me general anesthetic. He relented and gave me an epidural because I cried, "I want to be awake when my baby is being born!" Glenn was present in the delivery room. As our tiny baby Rachael was laid on my chest, I was overwhelmed by how much God had blessed me.

Those who were close to us wondered how I could possibly

take care of baby Rachael. I wondered that myself. The first time I tried to dress her, I wound up in tears because my hands couldn't fasten the snaps on her tiny sleepers.

When I cried out to my mother, "No two-week old baby was going to get the best of me." Mom decided to replace all those snappers with Velcro fasteners. I was very determined to develop ways to give Rachael the best care possible.

Glenn worked nights when Rachael was an infant, so he

struggled to balance getting enough rest and helping me take care of her during the day. Glenn was great at playing with her outside, particularly taking her on walks or going to the convenience store for ice cream.

When she got older, Glenn and I noticed Rachael's interest in music. She loved to listen to her Daddy play his guitar. She inherited her father's musicianship, and she started to play the flute in the fifth grade.

When Rachael was three and four years old, I took advantage of her desire to be "Mommy's little helper" by putting some of the unbreakable dishes in the cupboards so she could reach what she needed.

I tried to make home as normal as possible. I didn't have the option of using my hands to entertain and discipline her. So, I had to find other ways, such as giving her a stern look or playing games with her. Rachael remembers, "When Mom wanted me to hurry and get dressed she would play games with me. 'I'm going to beat you getting ready,' she'd tease. Even when I figured out that I could always win because Mom was always slow, I still hurried. When I got old enough to understand Mom's main objective, I realized we both won."

Sometimes when Rachael disobeyed my instructions we both wound up in predicaments. For instance, when she was about eight years old, she wanted to use a curling iron with combs attached. I told her not to do this because I knew it would get twisted up in her hair. Rachael went ahead, and soon discovered why I said, "Don't do that." She had to go to a neighbor to get the curling iron untangled.

Chapter 6

As **Rachael grew older, I could see something had** to change because Glenn and I were arguing more and more frequently. I tried to stop Glenn from yelling when Rachael was home, but I didn't always succeed. "Sometimes I did hear them at it in their bedroom at night," Rachael recalls.

Besides counseling at Good Samaritan Ministries, I gained a lot of support through attending a self-help group. My ears perked up one day when the teacher described the abuse cycle. She taught that after a person gets angry and apologizes, he may do well for a while. That's the honeymoon period. Typically, the spouse begins to hope that there won't be any more fighting. But the cycle begins again when the tension between the couple builds, and the spouse is blamed and battered again.

I took a number of classes on boundaries. I frequently heard was that my behavior affected his, but that was true only to a point. Many episodes were completely unprovoked. One pleasant evening together, Glenn's mood suddenly changed drastically.

When I asked him what was wrong, he answered, "I heard you laughing at me."

This kind of behavior had been going on for a number of years. One day, I told my counselor about the incident. He picked up a medical reference book and read aloud the description of a condition that sounded very familiar. When I heard that the condition could only be controlled by medication, it was like finding the missing piece to a puzzle and gave me the strength to take some very difficult steps. Glenn refused to take medication, but I knew I had to make my daughter's safety and well-being my priority. After years of trying to keep our family together, I made the heart-breaking decision to get a divorce.

When my marriage ended I learned that, whether one was experiencing marital pain or the frustration of living with a disability, the stages of grief were the same. In addition, I thought if I tried harder in both situations, things would change. They did: they got worse!

Finally, I had to accept the fact that nothing I did would change either situation. It's like me trying to walk straight. I can try all I want and maybe walk straight for a little bit, but my efforts won't change the fact that I have Cerebral Palsy.

I was fortunate to have friends and family, including my church family, to support me through the process. I grew stronger as my relationship with the Lord deepened. I gained inspiration and strength through reading the Bible and the writings of Oswald Chambers. Eventually, I began to learn that God can heal even the most broken places in our hearts.

It took time and lots of help from God, but gradually I did begin to heal from my divorce. At Bettie Mitchell's invitation, I joined Good Samaritan Ministries. I took the lay counseling classes they offered. I then went on to volunteer as a counselor and co-lead a recovery group. I was thrilled to discover that I had found my perfect fit! Although one of my dreams was helping people with disabilities, it was a joy to encourage people who I consider to be among the *walking wounded.*

For several years GSM raised money to educate and train needy people in Africa by having a Treasures Sale. Rather than bring items we didn't want any longer, we were asked to contribute things that were precious to us. It was at one of those sales that I was reminded that God can use our physical pain to our advantage. As I was getting ready to leave the sale, I lost my balance and ran into a wall.

This is one of my most stupid falls ever! I thought, disgusted with myself. But at least I had a soft landing so I didn't think I was hurt. Then, when I tried to stand up, my left foot screamed, "I don't like the way you landed on me!"

An x-ray revealed that I'd broken a bone in my foot, meaning I had to give up my treasured independence during the Treasures

Sale. The irony wasn't lost on me as I had to lean on many friends from church and GSM for support during my recovery.

A few months later I was by myself and I fell again. I was able to get up and forgot all about my fall, but the next day I noticed an unusual twinge whenever I turned my head. Two days later, I was in terrible pain. When I tried to make breakfast, I poured my coffee all over the counter. Even putting a spoon in my mouth hurt.

I moped around trying to summon enough energy to go to a meeting I had scheduled. Finally, I realized I couldn't make it. In desperation, I called my chiropractor, who I saw routinely.

"Did you fall again?" he asked as he entered the examining room.

I nodded. It took several treatments to make me pain-free. "I'm amazed that you heal as well as you do," the doctor commented. Although I knew he wanted to encourage me, my inner voice said, "You're getting old." I'd fallen down so many times that my body was beginning to pay the price.

My neck injury brought with it a heightened sense of vulnerability. To ignore my fears about the possibility of living in pain was as effective as sticking out my arm to protect myself from the impact of an oncoming car. I reminded myself, however, that God hadn't given me a spirit of fear but of power and might and a sound mind. I'd simply have to count on Him.

Chapter 7

When Glenn left home for the last time, Rachael was very confused and as a result, became very angry with me. "I'd made a coupon book for Mom's birthday right after he left home the last time," Rachael remembers. "The divorce made me so angry that I ripped it up. I even kicked a hole in the wall—I was strong from pushing Mom in her wheelchair."

Eventually, Rachael began to understand why I had divorced her father and she relaxed because there was more stability at home. Rachael's father visited her weekly and showed that he really cared about her.

Despite our struggles, Rachael never felt sorry for herself. She often recited the line from one of her favorite books, *I'll Love You Now and I'll Love You Forever.*

Meanwhile I continued to grieve. To me, a normal life meant having a happy marriage. I so wanted to be successful at it and divorce meant giving up that dream. That tragedy was compounded a hundred-fold when my Dad, who'd suffered from lung problems for years, died from emphysema the day I made the decision to file.

I remained determined that Rachael would live as normal a life as possible. She had friends in our apartment complex. They played ball in a nearby field, on the basketball court and rollerbladed in open spaces. I can't drive, so I depended on friends, the Tri-Met Lift, and the paratransit system to take us where we needed to go. When we just wanted to get out of the house, Rachael pushed my wheelchair around our apartment complex while chatting or I quizzed her on her math problems and spelling words.

In many instances we worked as a team. When Rachael had a softball game, she would help me get into my wheelchair. Then I balanced the cooler containing our lunch and other paraphernalia on my lap while Rachael pushed my chair.

Since people didn't usually volunteer to help, Rachael learned to accept pushing my wheelchair everywhere. "One ball field I hated was up a big hill," she remembers. "Pushing Mom's wheelchair was *hard.*"

Most of the time, strangers didn't realize that I was Rachael's mom. Once when she was a toddler, I went to the grocery store with a neighbor and her daughter, also named Rachael. When the clerk asked my friend's daughter her name, she said it was Rachael. She then asked my daughter her name and got the same response.

"Boy! Your mom must like the name Rachael." She was shocked when my daughter looked at me and said, "No, *this* is my Mom."

People often assume that Cerebral Palsy has affected my mental capacities as well. It always irritated me when they referred to me in the third person—the way an airline hostess once did when she asked my companion, "Does she know how to fasten her seat belt?"

Rachael hated it when it was her turn to call someone for a ride to church or one of her ballgames. "Mom did it until I was old enough. Two positive results are that I learned to ask for what I need and how to give good directions."

Chapter 8

Everyone **has wounds in their hearts triggered by** people we encounter. One spring day Colleen, my long-time home health aide and friend, took me to the grocery store. I used an electric shopping cart to weave through the aisles. When I was finished, I drove up to the checkout counter. The cashier looked at Colleen. "Does she want paper or plastic?"

Colleen rolled her eyes as if to say, *Here we go again.* She looked at me. "What type of bag do you want?"

I felt an emotional landmine triggering, but I smiled as I looked at the clerk. "Paper, please."

Her shocked expression almost threw me into a laughing spasm until she continued in a high pitched voice. "Wow, dear. You filled up your whole basket." As she rang up my groceries, she continued. "Can you cook?"

"Yes. I can fix several things." I nodded my head at Colleen. "She helps me with tasks I can't do."

As she put the fourth box of granola bars in my bag, she spotted all the Capri Suns. "I can see the kinds of snacks you enjoy. Honey, you are all stocked up."

"Actually it's my turn to take snacks to my daughter's softball team. The girls really enjoy them, so I'm glad that everything was on sale."

I could see by the look on her face that something had finally registered with her. Her voice suddenly became conversational. "Oh! I have girls in softball, too." While she finished ringing up the total, I handed Colleen my debit card. "Will you take care of this part?" When we finished the transaction, I smiled at the clerk. "Have a good day!"

"You too. Maybe I'll see you at a game sometime."

"We'll see," I called over my shoulder as I drove my cart away.

When we were outside the store, I erupted. "Let's get out of here. I can't believe how ticked off I still get when someone acts as though I'm invisible."

"No kidding! You looked like a volcano about to erupt!"

"I felt as though she'd nailed me inside a box and I had to fight my way out of it!" I lamented.

I don't like these feelings, but they're opportunities for God to comfort and heal my heart.

Chapter 9

Rachael learned to be enterprising and a team player at the early ages of three and four. I kept dishes we used on low shelves so I could reach them. Whenever our dishes and cooking supplies were out of reach, she climbed up like a monkey and handed them down to me. Our portable dishwasher was in a closet, so Rachael helped me push it over to the sink and hook it up to the faucet.

When Rachael was quite a bit younger, I played with her on the floor so she didn't become alarmed when I fell. On her third birthday, she received a battery operated school bus. Whenever I came into the room and she was playing with it, she'd cry and stand between me and the bus. Finally, I realized she was afraid the bus might run into me. I knew I couldn't stop her from worrying about me, but I could teach her that I would be okay if I did fall.

It was especially challenging to stay one step ahead of a fast-moving little one when she didn't want to do what she was told. One story Rachael likes to tell is when she ran away from home because she didn't want to take a nap. "I packed my Barbie suitcase and went to a friend's house on the other side of the apartment complex. When I showed up at my friend's house, her mom called my mother. Mom told her, 'Put that girl to work!' That woman had a pile of clothes that needed to be folded. What's more, she wouldn't even let me talk to my friend."

Later that day, Rachael returned home and knocked on our door. I was glad she was home until she said, "I'm going to get my bike." I took a deep breath and replied flatly, "Oh, no. That's for the little girl who lives here." Those words were so hard to say I felt like I was going to choke, but I knew I couldn't let her have it. Rachael recalls, "When Dad got home from work he came over to get me. Boy was I in trouble! It was the first time I was ever grounded."

Many times Rachael did things other kids her age didn't need to think about. One evening early in December when Rachael was about nine, we were on her bed snuggling under a favorite blanket while she read aloud a Christmas story. When she finished, she looked at me and asked, "When are we going to decorate for Christmas?"

I would have loved to say: "Let's do it together right now." But when I thought of all the boxes of decorations stored away, I knew it would be too much to do by ourselves. I told her we had to wait until someone was here to help us.

A moment later, she jumped up. "Don't come out until I tell

you." I sat there wondering what in the world she was up to. Several moments later, she proudly led me into the living room. All by herself, she'd dug out our small artificial tree and set it up.

When Rachael was a little girl, I asked my friend Colleen to help me give our home a festive flare. When Rachael grew older, the majority of the decorations stayed in the closet. I set up my nativity and the nice decorations my Mom made for me throughout the years. It has become freeing to bring out just a few of my favorite things.

Through the years, I had to learn how to find ways to wrap gifts and fix a nice meal on Christmas with my limitations. Wrapping presents was a task I always had to pawn off on someone else. When I thought about the fact that the paper was ripped off in seconds, I decided to replace it with an easier option, gift bags.

Instead of being upset because I can't cook special foods for Christmas Eve dinner, I selected a menu that my caregiver could prepare ahead of time. When Rachael became old enough to drive, one of our favorite things to do was order a nice meal from a nearby restaurant.

When I learned shortcuts to preserve my sanity, I found myself enjoying the season a thousand percent more.

When Rachael was about eight, we flew to Montana to spend

Christmas with my family. "I carried a huge backpack," Rachael recalls. "It was full of both of our books and my coloring books and crayons, snacks, doll and other supplies. Mom was in a wheelchair and I pushed it through the airport with the backpack on her lap."

Rachael still remembers that when we were on the way, someone looked down at me and asked, "Did you get a dolly for Christmas?"

When I think about it, I recall just wanting to slap her.

Rachael also remembers that Grandma became her teacher during those visits. "She made me do math and taught me how to cut my meat and twist spaghetti around my fork and slurp it in. Grandma was full of surprises. One time she jumped on the bed with me as we sang the *Five Little Monkeys.* I followed her everywhere. She called me her shadow."

Rachael's mind was always working. When she wondered if she could hatch chicks from eggs, she hid them under her bed where she thought they'd be warm. Grandma was the one who discovered her stash on a visit from Montana. Rachael was disappointed that her experiment failed.

$\mathcal{R}$achael attended a Christian school until the seventh grade. When I saw the enrollment decline and heard rumors it was closing, I began to look for other options. Friends advised me that Rachael would be fine in public school because she'd had a good start. Nevertheless, I was nervous about her transition until the Lord calmed my fears.

When I gazed at a tree outside our apartment window, God seemed to say that Rachael would be like that tree. I recalled Scripture about oaks of righteousness with roots that go down deep. So, she went from a small Christian school to a public one.

"Fortunately, I found a good group of friends quickly," Rachael recalls. But I remained a hands-on parent while she was in middle-school and high-school. One evening, when she was in high school, I was surprised when she said, "Remember the night of the science fair we went to in middle school? I actually ditched you when I left you with your friends because I was afraid of what my friends would say. I accepted your condition as normal, but I knew my friends' would think it was abnormal."

I didn't realize she'd done that, until she told me several years later.

Sometimes Rachael also resented the extra care she had to give me. But she often asked herself: "Who else is going to do it? Besides, when I helped Mom, we both were able to do things quicker."

I was very fortunate to have friends who had kids in the same activities as Rachael and who took me to many of the events. After Rachael's first band competition, I went home and expected her to follow. She had called to ask if she could go over to her friends. Unfortunately, I didn't get the call, and I got worried when she didn't come home. When I found out where she was, I sent one of my friends to pick her up. Of course she was mad, but she didn't do anything like that again!"

Although Rachael had natural musical ability from a young age, when her dad and I tried to get her to play an instrument, she didn't want to do the work. Much to my delight, in fifth grade Rachael learned to play the flute and did so in the school band.

When Rachael was in her senior year of high school, I began worrying about how I could possibly send her to college. I knew there were scholarships available, but how could I possibly find out if there were ones for which she was eligible? Once again I prayed for God's help.

A few days later, Rachael came home from running an errand and told me that her friend Sarah knew someone who helped low-income families find funding to send their kids to college. Sarah gave Rachael his phone number. I gave her a hug. "Wow! Now *that's* an answer to prayer. Let's call and make an appointment."

At the meeting, the financial planner explained the process. Afterward, our heads were full of things he wanted us to do, but I was so excited. "Rachael, I think Mike will really be able to help us."

"But Mom, I want to go to George Fox College like you did. It's a Christian school, and my favorite instructor from high school teaches band there now. But Mike says there isn't enough money available for a private college. They're too expensive."

"Don't worry. If God wants you to go there, He'll open the door." I reminded her of my own experience. "Chaplain Ron told me that if it was God's will, He would make a way." After we prayed together, I had the assurance that it was in God's hands. "He has a plan for you just as He did for me," I told her.

Rachael realized that, while her only obstacle was money, I had faced other barriers. "How did God get you from Montana to college in Oregon, anyway? I bet Grandma was nervous about having you so far from home." When we talked about all the obstacles I overcame, she relaxed.

The next time we met with Mike, and he read the summary of Rachael's high school activities. "My word! How have you managed to do so many things?"

She grinned. "When I was a kid I wanted to play softball, and Mom discovered that I was eligible for scholarships through the Little League Association. When I entered high school, she found scholarships that enabled me to participate in extracurricular activities. In fact, my first two years of high school, I was on two softball teams and in band."

"You're just the kind of student we like to help."

Besides keeping up with her homework and other activities, Rachael filled out several scholarship applications. After checking the mailbox daily for months, she ran in one day waving an open envelope. "Mom, listen to this. It's from the Ford Foundation. Over twenty-three hundred students applied for a scholarship, and I'm one of the two hundred they want to interview. If I'm chosen, they'll pay for ninety percent of unmet financial needs to any school in Oregon!"

When we arrived for the interview a few months later, it looked as though the building was inaccessible to wheelchairs. I turned to Rachael. "Honey, you go ahead in. I'll just wait in the car."

"No, Mom! You have been my main support all along. I want you to wait inside where the other mothers are." After a bit of persistence, we figured out where the wheelchair entrance was. Looking sharp in a pin-striped suit her grandmother bought, Rachael went in for the interview while I waited with the other mothers.

The great news is Rachael was awarded a Ford Family scholarship. It paid for ninety percent of her undergraduate degree and eighty percent of her Master's degree. She lived on campus and was in the music program that included a choral group that presented Christmas concerts. In her junior year, she did a flute recital and in her senior year, she performed a recital titled "Compilation of Sounds" in which she played the flute and sang. Everyone knew she played the flute, but they were shocked when they heard her lovely singing voice.

I can only shake my head when I recall how I choked back tears when Rachael conducted the college band at her graduation. My brother leaned over and grinned. "This is supposed to be a happy occasion."

My mother and I smiled up at him. "These are tears of joy!"

After getting her master's degree, Rachael settled into her career as an elementary music teacher. One evening she told me that she had gone out for coffee with her friend, Vince. They had known each other for two years because they were both on the worship team at church. But suddenly, sparks began to fly between them, and there was no putting out the fire!

I wasn't fooled when Rachael came home and said casually, "We went out for coffee and agreed to take our relationship really slowly."

The next day she reported, "We're going together."

I knew they were on the fast track.

They began dating in the summer and were engaged on Christmas Eve 2012.

Going together to shop for the wedding dress was a special mother/daughter experience for Rachael and me. While I couldn't help in the same ways other moms could, Rachael was well-organized and planned her March wedding using lots of Pinterest ideas for decorations.

Their venue was a restored barn that shone with lights and tulle. Pastor Roy from Joni & Friends performed the ceremony, and everything turned out beautifully. Rachael was positively glowing as she walked down the aisle. I knew it was a day of endings and new beginnings, as I felt myself releasing her to Vince.

Chapter 11

It was a bright spring morning when my friend, Barb, stopped by to give me a ride to a weekly prayer group called Moms in Touch. We had become friends soon after the school year began when we discovered that our daughters were in the same eighth grade class.

On the way, Barb asked if I could chaperone the class's trip to the zoo. "We need one more person."

Her request surprised me. "That might be difficult because I have trouble walking," I told her. "The only way I can keep up is if I take my scooter."

"No problem. There are lots of hills at the zoo. You can use it to chase the kids. That will make it easier on the rest of us."

After I agreed, Barb said that she and her husband would load my scooter into their van the night before. "I'll just swing by your house and pick you up in the morning."

They unloaded my scooter at the zoo the next morning and

Barb glanced at me as she filled the basket with stuff for the picnic. "Hey, this is pretty handy. You can carry this for us!"

When the busload of excited eighth graders arrived, we began our tour. Everything worked like clockwork. After the kids had seen all the animals and eaten the picnic lunch, we breathed a sigh of relief.

When we finished packing up, Barb suggested that I drive my scooter close to the door of the van and I did so. Before getting off the scooter, I looked at Barb. "Watch my hand." Her gaze dropped from my face to my left hand. "When you want to go forward, pull this lever toward you with all your fingers. Push here with your thumb to make it go backward."

After helping me board the van, she hopped on my scooter. But within seconds she called out anxiously: "How do I make it stop?"

"Let go!"

My directions didn't seem to register so she repeated her question with panic in her voice. "How do I make it stop!"

I called out more loudly. "Let go!"

Clearly, Barb was panicking. This time she screamed. "Help! How do I make it stop?"

When my scooter was within inches of hitting her shiny new

van, I threw up my arms and yelled at the top of my lungs. "Raise your hands and let go!"

Finally, she understood. As she let go, the scooter stopped. She laughed. "Oh! You mean let go!"

After I got home and had time to reflect on the day, I realized that God had used our outing to show how fear can affect different people in different ways. Her fear prevented her from hearing what I was trying to tell her. My fear of rejection can keep me from enjoying life as completely as I might. But God is always willing to repeat His directions so we can take another tiny step of faith.

The other day I turned a year older and reflected on the previous year. Rachael and I went to a Joni and Friends camp and also took a trip to Montana to visit my folks. I began blogging. Even though it took me about two hours to get ready for each day, I learned to use some of that "wasted" time to listen to audio books.

Birthdays are like New Year's Day—a time to dream about what might happen in the coming year. But unless I plan ways to accomplish my dreams, they become casualties. As a result, I find myself wrestling with the feeling that I haven't accomplished much. So recently, I decided to examine my activities and see if they were helping me reach my goals.

The fear of failing to live up to my expectations has kept me from moving forward according to God's rhythm. Every time I surrendered my desire to accomplish things quickly, it was as though God took His scissors to my cycle of nonproductive busyness. When I let Him lead me one small step at a time, I get more done and have more fun.

Chapter 12

With the help of caregivers and my friends, I've been able to raise a daughter and live alone.

Colleen is like a family member because she's been my caregiver for twenty-five years. She has often gone out of her way to cheer me up. Several years ago after an operation, I was bored and my hospital bed seemed to be especially hard. Colleen surprised me by bringing Rachael to visit me. To be able to share ice cream with my little girl that afternoon was better than any medication my doctor could have ordered.

Although it may look like I'm the only one who benefits from our relationship, Colleen and I know that our relationship works because we treat each other as equals. Colleen frequently tells me how I encourage her and give her courage.

Asking people for help still feels humbling and threatening, so I resisted when Colleen suggested that I ask a few of my friends to come to my house so we could discuss how I could use their help more consistently. I finally agreed, and just a few weeks later,

Team Lyla was formed. Each woman on the team volunteered to help me once a month in a particular way. Most of them brought meals over while others did special projects. While my friends were helping me, I had the opportunity to encourage them.

JoAnne, Rachael and I at Disneyland, celebrating my birthday.

In December Jan, a friend who worked on special projects for me, decorated my quad cane with red and white stripes. I told everyone that my cane was my date for holiday activities. When she redecorated it after Christmas to look pretty and feminine, I renamed it "Stella." My cane never says a word, but it sure opens lots of conversations.

One of those conversations took place a week or so later when I flew to Montana. On my return flight, I had to change planes. Before I boarded the Seattle to Portland plane, I went to the restroom, and then to the boarding gate. That's when I noticed that Stella was missing. "I think I left my quad-cane in the last stall on the left," I told an airline employee. "It's decorated with turquoise ribbons and felt flowers."

I breathed a sigh of relief when she retrieved it for me. While the flight attendant helped me get settled in my seat, she commented, "I decorated my cane when I used one."

After she finished giving people their snacks and beverages, the flight attendant sat in the seat next to me and explained more of her story. "I was on my way to work and as I crossed the street a truck hit me and seven other people. One of them died. It took me over a year to recover."

Since she seemed to walk up and down the plane with ease, I assumed that she'd recovered completely. When I asked if she was okay now, I cringed at her response. "I live with chronic pain, and I'll have to have both knees replaced."

I shook my head, expressing my sympathy. How easy it is to make false assumptions about people and what they experience.

Chapter 13

When I'm at peace, I recall Paul's words about grace being sufficient for us and allow his words to soothe my soul. But when things go wrong, finding peace can be harder than holding onto a slippery bar of soap.

It was about ten one Saturday morning when Rachael told me that she and her roommates wanted to go to the art show in Portland. "Can we have lunch at your house before we leave?" she asked.

When I fix meals, I have to choose foods that I don't need to cut or take in or out of the oven. I also try to do as much as possible before guests arrive. As I pondered Rachael's request, I imagined my table set with my grandmother's flair—complete with delicately arranged sandwiches and trays of veggies.

Although I *knew* it was wishful thinking, I simply couldn't let go of it. The more irritated I became with my limitations, the more I could feel my stomach and my hands tighten. The harder I worked to get lunch ready, the more flustered I became. Even the "easy open" can of juice refused to cooperate. When I did finally get it open, some of the contents decorated my face as well as the ceiling.

I was a mess and nothing was ready when Rachael and her friends arrived. She greeted me with an amused look. "What in the world happened?" After hearing a rundown of my morning, she comforted me. "Mom, it's okay. Just go wash the juice off your face and I'll finish getting lunch ready."

Later I realized that I'd wanted to ignore my limitations and prove myself as capable as anyone else. When that didn't happen, I became angry. I didn't realize at the time that God was continuing to take me into even deeper healing.

I hadn't forgotten my experiences the next morning when I sat in church and listened to a friend tell the congregation: "The Lord healed my knee. Now I can ride my bike again." Like a volcano letting off plumes before an eruption, my heart screamed, *What about me, Lord?* Her praise report sounded ridiculous. I couldn't cook because of my hands, and she was worried about riding her bike!

At the end of the service when the pastor asked people to come up for prayer, I felt as though I was inside God's pressure cooker. Asking for prayer seemed extremely difficult. Usually, when I was confronted with something I couldn't do, I figured out a solution. But for the past two days, I'd been an angry mess. I was ashamed and embarrassed and was tempted to go home. Yet, if I didn't ask for help, I felt as though I'd explode.

When Pastor James finished praying with people who had gone forward, he started to walk toward the exit of the sanctuary. I asked a friend to go get him.

He greeted me with a question. "What's going on?"

I struggled to explain the amount of turmoil I felt. "My life gets so frustrating sometimes."

I wondered what reaction would my confession bring?

He smiled. 'Well, I imagine it does." He talked quietly with me and prayed. I left the sanctuary reassured. It was by surrendering my feeble efforts to achieve the impossible and receive God's grace moment by moment that even someone with Cerebral Palsy can experience peace.

Not being able to drive or get where I need to go is one of the inconveniences of having Cerebral Palsy. But even when my plans don't work, God always uses it for my good.

On one occasion I needed to go to Salem—the state capitol of Oregon—to testify in the legislature. I made arrangements with a friend to take me there, but she got sick the night before. So I spent that night and all the next morning trying to find a ride. I actually made it to Salem about two minutes before my appointment, awed at my Father's faithfulness

When it comes to getting around, I *can* walk, although doing so is difficult. But when I go shopping, a wheelchair makes the trip much more enjoyable. When Rachael and I went to one of her favorite clothing stores, she piled several outfits in my lap to try on. Then she looked for a place where my chair wouldn't be in the way while she tried on the outfits. Satisfied that she had done that, she went into the dressing room. A few minutes later, when she came out to show me one of the outfits, Rachael was confronted by the sales clerk, who told Rachael tersely, "You'll have to move *her* out of the way."

Both of us were stunned by her demand since we were the only ones in the department.

I felt as though the salesclerk was ripping off my scab, revealing the raw wound of being teased and dismissed throughout the years. My heart screamed: "I'm so sick of this." But I knew if I yelled at the clerk, I would only look worse, so all I could say was: "Hurry up. We need to get out of here."

I was unhappy with myself as Rachael pushed my wheelchair to the checkout counter.

She whispered in my ear: "Mom! Are you alright?"

I simply nodded, wishing that encounters like this got easier with time. But after all these years, I was still vulnerable. That experience was one more reminder that I would always be totally dependent on God for grace in time of need. It wasn't until I stopped going around in circles that I could move forward in His peace.

Chapter 14

Years ago I attended a Joni and Friends event in California. Joni Eareckson Tada became paralyzed from the neck down after a diving accident as a teenager. Since then, she has devoted her life to helping others affected by disabilities hear the Gospel of Jesus Christ and live for Him.

Except for part of my childhood when I went to school with kids with disabilities, I wasn't usually around very many other disabled people. Attending that first conference was life-changing. I felt like I found a forgotten piece of myself and embraced myself wholly.

In 2013, I attended again, this time as part of the organization's volunteer area ministry. In March 2014 I was selected to be the area director of the Portland (Oregon) Chapter of Joni and Friends.

I also actively participated in Border Mountain, a nonprofit organization , founded by JoAnne Chitwood, a hospice nurse, when she experienced personal tragedy. JoAnne and I met at Good

Samaritan Ministries where we both were counselors and were co-leaders of a recovery group.

Later, JoAnne moved to St. Croix and dedicated herself to help hurting people find emotional and spiritual growth and healing regardless of religious background, race or creed. Her purpose is to provide a safe and nurturing environment to process personal grief and loss. Individuals also work to improve interpersonal communication skills, identify and correct dysfunctional family programming, and learn to live a more peaceful and serene life.

I have co-facilitated healing-after-loss groups with my friend JoAnne at these retreats for the past several years. Besides having some fun activities, we spend a portion of each day meeting as a group. JoAnne presents material from the workbook she developed, and each person has the opportunity to tell their story. It always amazes me how much healing is brought to each participant through this process.

For many years, JoAnne persisted in challenging me to come to St. Croix and help facilitate classes. My initial response was that mobility issues made it unlikely, if not too complicated. A month before my daughter's wedding, JoAnne called again and said, "Tickets are cheaper right now and several of our friends are coming over to the island. Why don't you come with them?" The next thing I knew, I had my ticket!

Colleen & I at St. Croix

When I finally took the risk and made the flight with Colleen and my friend Julie, God rewarded me in so many ways. First of all, I was able to tell my story and encourage others who were struggling to move forward in their lives. I actually had spent several years before this seeking inner-healing, both privately with a counselor and in groups. Years before this particular retreat, I experienced a great deal of healing when I led my first retreat with JoAnne. There were two amputees in the group, so it was a special time of sharing and emotional healing for all of us.

Then there was the beauty of St. Croix itself. On one occasion, our hotel was right on the beach, so my friends could walk me to the water's edge. While the place was breathtaking, I still felt a sting of sadness because I couldn't join my friends when they went out to swim and snorkel. This time, however, instead of ignoring the way I felt, I told my Heavenly Father, and I received His comfort. Then I could focus on what I could do instead of dwelling on what I couldn't do. My friends helped me get into the water. When they went horseback riding, I even sat sidesaddle on a horse for a few seconds!

I discovered one of my favorite things to do is sitting in a lawn chair soaking up the warm sunshine with my feet in the beautiful blue water. In the stillness, God reminded me of words in Psalm 18:19. "He rescued me, because He delighted in me."

Athletes gathered to participate in St. Croix's 25th annual triathlon. I sat on the boardwalk in my wheelchair watching everything. When the athletes swam toward shore to finish the first leg of the competition, they were already tired and thankful to have a little bit of help from two men who were squatting down at the shoreline. Just when the swimmers were within arm's length of the shore, two helpers linked arms with them so they could go on to the next part of the competition. As the athletes ran to grab their bikes, those who had helped them out of the water remained at their post to help other swimmers.

That's when I noticed a father with two young daughters dressed in matching shorts and tee-shirts. They were sitting on the boardwalk where all the swimmers were getting out of the water. As they patiently waited for a glimpse of their mom, who was a competitor, the older little girl held a sign that said "GO MOMMY GO!" and the younger girl held a brightly decorated sign that said "WE LOVE YOU!" That's when I realized that helpers and spectators each played an important role in ensuring the success of the athletes.

It's easy to downplay the supportive role we have in life, but the athletes would have lost a lot of time if the helpers decided to leave their posts because they suddenly wanted to participate as athletes too. Those at water stations, in the medical tent, ones who gave directions at crucial junctions in the race, were all indispensable. Not only would the athletes have lost time, they may not have been able to complete the race at all.

In Ephesians, the apostle Paul talks about how each of us has a significant role in the Body of Christ. At times, we downplay the role we have and want a different one. I have certainly done that. But if we don't accept and use the gifts God does give us, it weakens the entire Body. I've found that as I've accepted the gifts

I've been given, it brings strength to everyone around me.

Just as the all the athletes and their support teams worked together to accomplish a single goal, Jesus Christ has called each of us to contribute our gifts, whatever they are, whether we are in a supporting role or in a lead role for the strengthening of the whole Body.

Again, my time in St. Croix definitely was not all work. We enjoyed the vegetation and culture of the land as well as a variety of outdoor activities. We were even able to witness the aurora borealis.

Despite my misgiving, I have learned to love travel. Years ago I went on the trip of a lifetime with Good Samaritan Ministries. I traveled to Poland, Egypt, and Israel. Many people assume my physical limitations would have made a trip like this impossible, but I had plenty of help. Sometimes men in our group carried me on their backs when the sites were particularly difficult to reach.

In Poland, we visited Auschwitz-Birkenau. I cringed feeling the effects of evil as soon as I stepped off the bus. The blind and handicapped were always the group of people to be put into Hitler's ovens. I peered into the display of a room full of crutches, and realized I would have been the first to go to the oven. I had often feared being disenfranchised and cast aside. I saw in front of me something far worse.

I also learned that, in Poland, if a woman's husband dies, she doesn't receive any income. So, I was especially impressed when our widowed hostess took a gift of food out of her cupboard and gave it to me. With that gesture, she demonstrated that, when you give from the little you have, it comes from the heart, and God will use it to bless others.

In Egypt, I had the delightful experience of riding on a camel. Camels are easier to ride than horses because they aren't as wide! Best of all, my heart felt at home when I crossed the border from Egypt into Israel, and I touched the ground where Jesus walked.

Chapter 15

I bought a new calendar for 2014 and looked over the important events that took place in 2013. My precious daughter Rachael's wedding. Trips to St. Croix to participate in a grief retreat. A trip to Southern California for a Joni and Friends Leadership Retreat. The official start of the Joni and Friends Volunteer ministry in the Portland area.

Looking back at 2013, there were some gifts I certainly didn't ask for that year. When I am reeling from an unwanted "gift," I've learned that it's a good idea to wait and see how God turns it into a treasure.

After I move through the disappointment that comes with unwanted pain, I experience hope again. Hard times are like being in a dark tunnel. When you're in it, you can hardly see a few feet ahead of you. All you know is that you have to keep feeling your way forward even though you don't know where the tunnel leads. But when you do make it through, you are blessed with the beautiful view of a cherry orchard with the trees in full blossom and roses covering the hillside. It's like Jesus said: "If you then, who are evil, know how to give good gifts to your children, how much more will your Father who is in heaven give good things to those who ask him!"

When I'm in a pensive mood, I think back on my life with absolute gratitude. While there have been mountains and valleys to slog through, God has been with me all the way.

Not only can I share the message of hope with people I meet, I have a beautiful daughter I raised pretty much by myself, and now two wonderful grandchildren.

Because of the love and sacrifice of my supportive family and many years of physical therapy,

I *did* learn to walk.

I *have* been able to help others who need a hand.

I *have* recounted my journey in this book.

What's more, for more than five years I *have* been able to write a blog, http://morethanlegs.wordpress.com. Through scores of blog posts, I offer readers stories of real-life ups and downs sprinkled with humor, help and (usually!) lots of hope.

Yes, it *has* been hard to deal with life's deepest disappointments, but God used them to prompt me to surrender my will and accept His in exchange. Each struggle along the way has led to more freedom. I am and will be eternally grateful to God for weaving tragedy into the fabric of my life and for teaching me how to stand.

Made in the USA
San Bernardino, CA
09 August 2018